EXAMINING DESERT HABITATS

Zelda King

PowerKiDS press
New York

Published in 2009 by The Rosen Publishing Group, Inc.
29 East 21st Street, New York, NY 10010

First Edition

Editor: Joanne Randolph
Book Design: Kate Laczynski
Photo Researcher: Jessica Gerweck

Photo Credits: Cover, pp. 1, 5, 9, 11, 13 (bighorn sheep, rattlesnake, desert iguana, cactus wren, golden eagle, bee, butterfly, scorpion), 17 (mesquite seeds), 19, 21 (Joshua tree, beavertail cactus, black-tailed jackrabbit, coyote, regal horned lizard, greater roadrunner, great horned owl) Shutterstock.com; p. 7 © Clip Art; p. 13 (kangaroo rat) © www.istockphoto.com/Stephen Love; p. 13 (black widow spider) © www.istockphoto.com/ Loretta Hostettler; p. 13 (desert pupfish) © AnimalsAnimals.com; p. 15 © Wayne Lynch/AgeFotostock.com; pp. 17, 21 (mesquite tree, Mojave rattlesnake) © www.istockphoto.com/John Billingslea Jr.; p. 21 (black-tailed jackrabbit) © www.istockphoto.com/Steven Love; p. 21 (kit fox) © www.istockphoto.com/Tara Minchin; p. 21 (banded gecko) © www.istockphoto.com/Rusty Dodson; p. 21 (Costa hummingbird) © Charles Melton/ Getty Images.

Library of Congress Cataloging-in-Publication Data

King, Zelda.
  Examining desert habitats / Zelda King. — 1st ed.
    p. cm. — (Graphic organizers. Habitats)
  Includes index.
  ISBN 978-1-4358-2721-9 (library binding) — ISBN 978-1-4358-3125-4 (pbk.)
ISBN 978-1-4358-3131-5 (6-pack)
  1. Desert ecology—Juvenile literature. 2. Deserts—Juvenile literature. I. Title.
  QH541.5.D4K56 2009
  577.54—dc22
                                    2008028406

Manufactured in the United States of America

CONTENTS

WHAT IS A DESERT?

Does the word "desert" make you imagine a hot, dry, sandy place? That is what many people think of, but it is only partly right.

Any very dry place is a desert, no matter how hot or sandy it is. Most deserts get less than 10 inches (25 cm) of **precipitation** yearly. Yet desert **habitats** are home to many living things.

Would you like to learn more about these interesting habitats? Graphic organizers can help you. A **cycle** chart, for example, can show the cycle of plant life throughout the year. Use this book's graphic organizers to learn facts about deserts!

Deserts are hard places to live, but many plants and animals live there, including people. This is a small village in the Thar Desert in India.

5

WHERE IN THE WORLD?

Deserts are found all over the world. They cover about one-fifth of Earth's land. That is an area bigger than all of North America!

The largest desert area runs across northern Africa and into central Asia. Three famous deserts are found here. They are the Sahara, the Gobi, and the Arabian Desert.

A famous desert called the Kalahari Desert is in southern Africa. Much of Australia is desert. The Atacama Desert runs along South America's western coast. Western North America has four big deserts. They are the Great **Basin**, the Mojave Desert, the Sonoran Desert, and the Chihuahuan Desert.

Deserts are shown in orange on this map. Antarctica is the world's largest desert, and the Sahara, in Africa, is the next largest.

Map: Deserts of the World

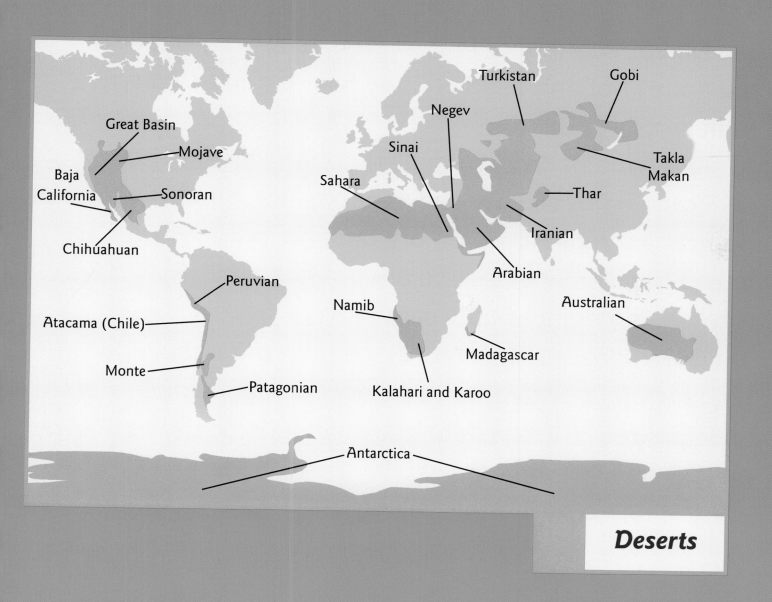

Great Basin

Mojave

Baja
California

Sonoran

Chihuahuan

Peruvian

Atacama (Chile)

Monte

Patagonian

Sahara

Namib

Kalahari and Karoo

Sinai

Negev

Turkistan

Gobi

Takla
Makan

Thar

Iranian

Arabian

Madagascar

Australian

Antarctica

Deserts

NOT ALL DESERTS ARE ALIKE

Do you remember that all deserts are dry but they are not all hot and sandy? There are actually four types of deserts.

One type of desert is called hot and dry. These deserts are hot all year and very hot in summer. **Semiarid** deserts are much like hot, dry deserts, but they do not get as hot. Coastal deserts are not hot at all. They have warm summers and cool winters.

Some deserts are actually cold! Some people do not know that Antarctica is a desert because it receives so little precipitation. Antarctica is the coldest place on Earth!

This compare/contrast chart shows some ways that different kinds of deserts are alike and different. All deserts have some rain, but can you find the only one that gets snow?

Compare/Contrast Chart: Types of Deserts

	Hot	Warm	Cold	Rain	Snow	Sandy Soil	Rocky Soil	Fine Soil	Heavy Soil
Hot and Dry	X			X		X	X	
Semiarid	X			X		X	X	X	
Coastal		X		X				X	
Cold			X	X	X				X

A HARD PLACE TO LIVE

Imagine living in a place where it is more than 100° F (38° C) during the day and drops below 32° F (0° C) at night. Imagine living in a place where months or even years pass between rains. How do you think desert plants and animals do it?

Special **adaptations** help desert plants and animals stay alive. Many animals live in **burrows** to escape the heat. Some come out to search for food only at night, when it is cooler. Many plants have thick coverings to keep them from losing water. Some store water. Such adaptations are the secret to dealing with life in this hard habitat.

This bar graph and chart show how much rain commonly falls each month in the Mojave Desert. About how many inches of rain does this desert get each year?

Bar Graph and Chart: Average Monthly Precipitation in the Mojave Desert

Months	Precipitation
January	1 in.
February	1 in.
March	1 in.
April	0 in.
May	0 in.
June	0 in.
July	0 in.
August	0 in.
September	0 in.
October	0 in.
November	1 in.
December	1 in.

Precipitation in Inches

January February March April May June July August September October November December

Months

DESERT ANIMALS

At noon, you will not see many animals in a desert. They are hiding from the heat. The desert comes alive at night, though, when it is cooler. Many animals also come out after it rains.

You may think of camels when you think of desert animals. Most desert animals, such as snakes, lizards, bugs, and mice, are small, though. A few larger animals, such as coyotes, live in or on the edges of deserts.

Some deserts even have fish, if you can believe it. The tiny desert pupfish lives in pools and streams in the Mojave and Sonoran deserts.

A concept map shows how subjects are connected to each other. This one shows some of the desert animals from the different animal groups, such as fish and birds.

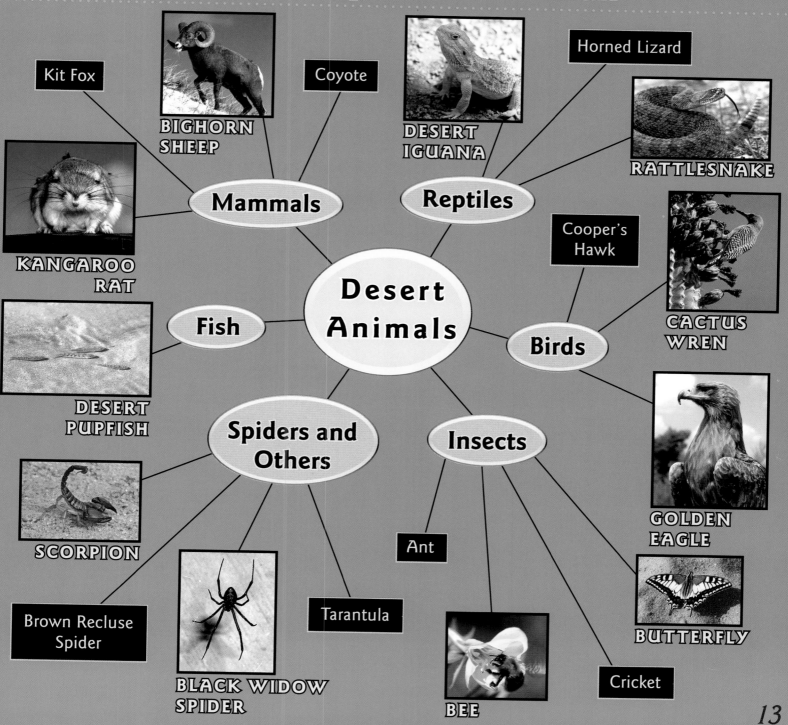

Concept Map: Desert Animals

Kit Fox

BIGHORN SHEEP

Coyote

DESERT IGUANA

Horned Lizard

RATTLESNAKE

Mammals

Reptiles

KANGAROO RAT

Cooper's Hawk

CACTUS WREN

Desert Animals

Fish

Birds

DESERT PUPFISH

Spiders and Others

Insects

GOLDEN EAGLE

SCORPION

Ant

Brown Recluse Spider

Tarantula

BUTTERFLY

BLACK WIDOW SPIDER

BEE

Cricket

A CLOSER LOOK:
THE DESERT TORTOISE

Do you know the difference between a turtle and a tortoise? A tortoise is simply a turtle that lives on land and cannot swim. Since tortoises live on land, they have legs and feet made for walking and digging, not swimming.

The desert tortoise lives in the Mojave and Sonoran deserts. Like other tortoises, it has a tall, rounded shell. It spends most of its life inside its many burrows to keep cool. When it does come out, it eats plants. It gets most of its water from these plants. A desert tortoise can live to be 100 years old!

This fishbone map organizes facts about the desert tortoise into four subjects. Can you use the map to find out what a desert tortoise likes to eat?

Fishbone Map: The Desert Tortoise

BODY

- Tall shell that is brown, gray, or black
- Shell is 9 to 15 inches (23-38 cm) long
- Thick legs, claws on feet
- Short tail

ADAPTATIONS

- Front legs have flat shape for digging
- Can store water in body for months
- Digs holes to hold rainwater
- Pulls head, legs, and tail inside shell to keep safe from enemies

DESERT TORTOISE

FOOD

- Grasses
- Wildflowers
- Bushes
- Cactus

ENEMIES

- Ravens
- Coyotes
- Foxes
- People

DESERT PLANTS

Unlike an animal, a desert plant cannot hide in a burrow or move around searching for water. Plants have other adaptations. They get water by sending their roots deep into the earth or spreading them out. They grow far apart so they are not trying to get the same water. A thick covering helps keep plants from losing water. **Spines** help keep animals from eating them.

Many kinds of plants have found ways to live in deserts. Cacti grow there. **Yuccas** and other plants with pointy leaves do, too. There are even trees, bushes, grasses, and wildflowers!

The mesquite tree is a common desert plant in America's Southwest. This sequence chart shows how a mesquite tree grows from a seed into a tree.

Sequence Chart: Growth of the Mesquite Tree

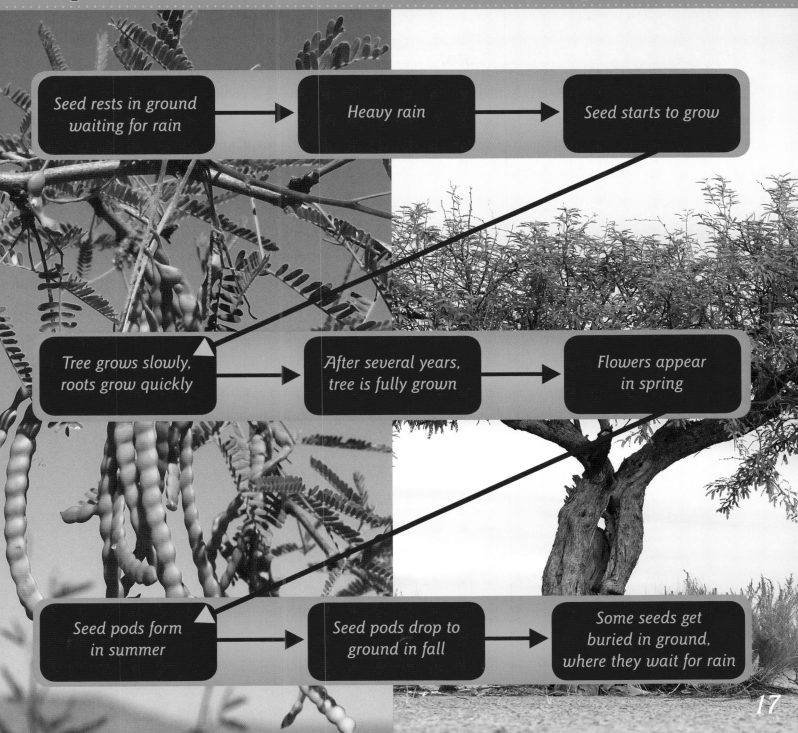

Seed rests in ground waiting for rain → Heavy rain → Seed starts to grow

Tree grows slowly, roots grow quickly → After several years, tree is fully grown → Flowers appear in spring

Seed pods form in summer → Seed pods drop to ground in fall → Some seeds get buried in ground, where they wait for rain

CONSIDER THE CACTUS

Did you know that there are about 2,000 kinds of cacti? Some of them can live 200 years! Cacti come in many shapes. Some look like bare trees, barrels, or pincushions. Cacti come in all sizes. The saguaro can be 60 feet (18 m) tall, while some cacti are less than 1 inch (2.5 cm) tall.

Cacti have thick skin covered by spines that help shade the plant. Some animals live in cacti or hide from their enemies there. Cactus stems, flowers, and fruit provide food and water for many animals. People get food from cacti, too. Cacti play a big part in the desert habitat!

A diagram tells you the parts that make something up. This diagram shows the parts of a prickly pear cactus.

Diagram: Parts of a Prickly Pear Cactus

FLOWER

STEM

FRUIT

SPINES

AREOLE

THE MOJAVE IS MIGHTY HOT

The Mojave Desert is the hottest place in the United States. The highest **temperature** ever recorded in the United States happened in the Mojave in 1913. It was 134° F (57° C)! The Mojave is also the driest place in the United States. Its valleys may get only 3 inches (8 cm) of rain yearly!

Most of the rain comes in winter, and the Mojave comes alive then. Hundreds of plants that rest most of the year grow and flower after the rains. The flowers draw butterflies, and the plants provide food for many desert animals. It is a special time in this hot, dry land.

This spider map lists some plants and animals that live in the Mojave Desert. Can you think of more plants and animals you could add to this map?

Spider Map: Life in the Mojave Desert

PLANTS

  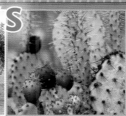

- *Joshua tree*
- Creosote bush
- *Mesquite tree*
- Mojave prickly pear
- *Beavertail cactus*

MAMMALS

- Black-tailed jackrabbit
- Desert woodrat
- *Coyote*
- Kangaroo rat
- *Kit fox*
- Mojave ground squirrel

LIFE IN THE MOJAVE DESERT

REPTILES

- *Banded gecko*
- Desert tortoise
- *Regal horned lizard*
- Desert iguana
- *Mojave rattlesnake*
- Mojave patchnose snake

BIRDS

- *Costa's hummingbird*
- LeConte's thrasher
- *Greater roadrunner*
- Ladder-backed woodpecker
- *Great horned owl*
- Cactus wren

21

PEOPLE AND DESERTS

For centuries, people got food and other things from deserts without hurting them. Today, though, deserts are in danger. People dump their trash in deserts. They farm in them and let their herds eat desert plants. People destroy deserts when they drive on them and build roads, houses, and other buildings. All these things hurt desert plants and animals. We must find ways to keep these beautiful and important habitats safe!

Can you think of ways to take care of deserts? Make a graphic organizer that shows these ways. Then use it to teach your friends how we can all help keep deserts safe!

GLOSSARY

adaptations (a-dap-TAY-shunz) Changes in an animal or plant that help it stay alive.

Antarctica (ant-AHRK-tih-kuh) The icy land at the southern end of Earth.

basin (BAY-sin) An area of land that slopes to a low place in the center.

burrows (BUR-ohz) Holes that animals dig in the ground for shelter.

cycle (SY-kul) Actions that happen in the same order over and over.

habitats (HA-beh-tats) The kinds of land where animals or plants naturally live.

precipitation (preh-sih-pih-TAY-shun) Any moisture that falls from the sky. Rain and snow are precipitation.

semiarid (seh-mee-A-rud) Having lower temperatures and cooler nights than hot, dry deserts.

spines (SPYNZ) Sharp, pointy things.

temperature (TEM-pur-cher) How hot or cold something is.

yuccas (YUH-kuz) Desert plants with long, stiff, pointed leaves and white flowers.

INDEX

WEB SITES

Due to the changing nature of Internet links, PowerKids Press has developed an online list of Web sites related to the subject of this book. This site is updated regularly. Please use this link to access the list:
www.powerkidslinks.com/graphoh/desert/